Life ‖‖‖‖‖‖‖‖‖ sit

Life In Transit

Celestial heart across the meridian space

H.S. PURE

© H. S. Pure, 2020

Published by Pure Lit

A CIP catalogue record for this book is available from the British Library.

ISBN 978-1-8382132-0-6

Book layout and cover design by Clare Brayshaw

Prepared and printed by:

York Publishing Services Ltd
64 Hallfield Road
Layerthorpe
York YO31 7ZQ

Tel: 01904 431213

Website: www.yps-publishing.co.uk

Contents

Part I: Heart So Pure   1

Part II: About the author   2

Part III: For You   3

Part IV: Inferior Heart   5

Part V: Superior Trust   111

Heart So Pure

HS Pure also known as, Heart So Pure is the author of Life In Transit.

He/she would like you to know that the words on these pages are for everyone who has felt the pain or sadness in the darkest moment of their life time.

Life is everlasting and will brighten your life in many ways but it is down to you, to try and take the leap across the distant sea and be free to shine bright amongst the stars.

About the author

I have felt pain and I have struggled at the hardest times, the amount of times I have chosen to give up and let myself down only because of the people around me.

They would always make me feel that I was never good enough.

With each laughter, with each point, it brought me down and before I knew it, many years had passed and I let my dreams just fly away.

Faith and trust was lost but most importantly, I forgot how to believe in myself.

My confidence was shattered into many pieces, though I try to still piece them together, my outer shell was just a shadow hiding the truth within.

So the journey began and I found myself on a path to see all the things happening around me and to many others what they endured, whether its' love, family or culture.

You have family, you work on your career, then money will come and love will follow.

What ever way you look at it, if it's not four it's three, if not three, then two, if not two, then 1, that one being you.

It's a start and I'm making every step to create a wonderful future.

HS Pure

For you

However, your life may be, wherever it may take
   you, don't let it put you down, look
Around, be strong. Life is just a stepping
   stone, whatever you wish for, could be
Right around the corner, just a few steps
   away. It is looking for you, trying to find you,
Missing you, I know things can be hard; I
   know people let you down, but believe
In yourself and never give up hope. Even
   when people laugh at you or point at you,
None of it matters; just believe in yourself
   like I believe in you. All you have is your
Dreams and your dreams can come true, you
   just have to believe it and never
Ever give up. I have been hurt, there has
   been many times I have given up but the
Right thing does come along and whisper
   in your ear to keep moving on.

Power to keep pushing on, this right thing is called Hope, it
   is a strong thing and it is all yours,
Understand that the world has not given up
   on you, your destiny lives on, you will
Rise through time. Become strong and
   experience so much more, in your life.
Everything in this world is a challenge; all
   you have to do is find the right
Way forward. One step at a time, love the
   stranger within, even if no one else does.
All the great people out there be strong, be
   brave, create that one special moment.
Leave all the worries behind and create
   those memories that will last forever.

Thank you

Inferior Heart

Inner beauty

In the darkest hour, there was a beauty
    Which exists only in the restless shadows
        It was unseen,
Like the shining angel
    Hidden from the world

We look, but we do not see
    Because we are enchanted by what it is
        We share a fear, which makes us afraid to see

Slowly, silently she fades.
    No more to be seen

I dream an idea, a thought within a thought
    A place to be free, a place to concur all
        To have the will to be free and to ask what I desired

    Only in a world beyond this one, all could be true
        A place to escape to and build hope
    To be free and to live a life beyond my own
To create that unexpected journey

    but I wonder back
        I cannot stay in this dream of wonder
            In this dream of peace and solitude
I always wake to something far better
    Someone who truly shows me what it feels to be truly alive

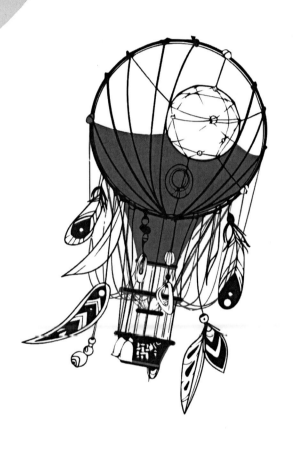

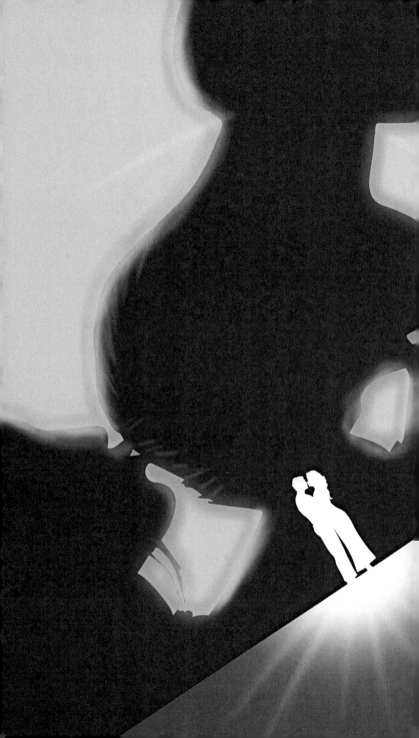

Care

There is only one thing that I believe in
That one uniqueness being you
You being the one that holds me close

I was surprised
Surprised to see you cared
Cared about the love we shared

There was one, that one being I
Who stood by you, who truly loves you
Always falling in love whenever we met

You were surprised
Surprised to see I cared
Cared about the love we shared
An endless passion never to end

Alone without you by my side
I lay here in my tears
Looking up at the sun
All I want is nothing more
Only to see your face once more

I shed my last tear
To show you my truth
A journey I must take
To prove my worth

I don't know where this road ends
I don't know when it will end
But I know, I will follow it
Wherever it will take me

I hungered for her touch that drives me everyday
Why does she take that extra step to show her love?
Why does she bite?
Every time

With so much passion, with so much care
With No fear
She always finds a way to attack without cause

She cuddles me with so much softness
Makes me feel safe, strong and relaxed
Then she bites when my guard is down

I don't know why she bites
But it just feels right

   She bites me because she loves me and so do I

I take her hand
And, look deep into her eyes
She does not speak
Yet I hear everything

It is my heart that calls upon your name
My breath is taken from me
Yet she does not speak
Yet she says nothing

Her heart beats, as does mine
I say nothing
But I hear everything
I am alone
Yet she speaks to my heart

My life is better ended, without my love
And if you love me, let your love fly to me

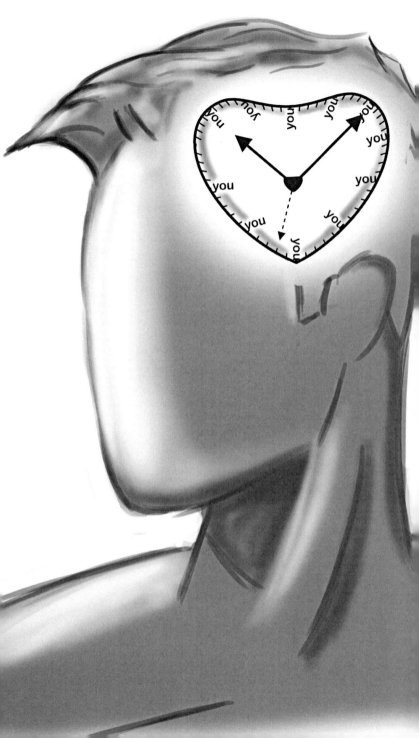

I do love you

I could listen to my heart
I could spend my life in this sweet pride
Even when I dream, you're on my mind

Who knows what tomorrow will bring
All I know is the way I feel
You're the last thing on my mind
When I fall asleep
And you are the first thing on my mind
When I wake

All we have is here and now
The road could be long at the end
But we have each other

Even when I dream again, I still miss you
I cannot explain this feeling
I don't know what this strange thing is
But I know this is where I belong

Here and now
I do know something
I do love you

This is you

Cause I'm kissing you
So deep and slow with the purest of my soul
You're sweet as honey.
With pride by your side
It makes you the purest of them all

Cause I'm touching you
My love is intertwined throughout time
You're soft as silk
as time goes by so slow, to become the fated ones
Watching these endless oceans together and forever

Cause I'm seeing you
Like a flower pointing in the right direction
You're white as milk
I see you, I feel you, with you looking into my eyes
I can see what I mean to you

Your love has touched me once and remained forever
Far across the ocean, I would travel full of money or none
We will still remain strong
With clear drops of beauty all rolled into one
To create you, my undying love

If I pay the price who knows what to expect
Can you lead me down that path?
Where I can think of you in my arms
It must have been cold in the shadows

I don't know, but I want you,
You are my hopeful; I fall ever so slowly over and over
again
Always seeing paradise
As the world around just changes, I will always love you
I think of making love, always with you

I'm standing forever with so much pride
To be the proud heart you choose
Because I'm so in love

Hold me tight and never let go
The feeling of love has touched my soul
I can say, "I was struck by a Cupid arrow"

I hope the heart that you choose
is the heart you will not lose.

Concrete wall

I've always wanted to tell you that I love you
But there has always been
That concrete wall between us
I wish I could hold you
And let the comfort of my arms
Tell you how I love you

I know they say
How can you love someone?
When you don't even know them
Maybe I can explain?
Maybe I cannot
But I do believe in love at first sight

I wish I could grab your heart
And tell you how much I love you
I wish you could feel
How much I care
I just want you to know of how I feel

If I did
It meant I got past this concrete wall
But I do not wish to lose our friendship
So I will stay quiet
And stay behind this wall

You

I hoped I'd fall in love with you
Every night in my dreams
I see you, I feel you

I lay here thinking of you
I look far and above, looking up into the sky
as I feel I'm drifting away

I'm hoping, wishing to see you
Thinking I may actually find you
But then I stop and realize
Nobody can find an angel like you

There goes my heart beating
It feels like this, when you look at me,
It's like there's no pain

What more can I say
To love someone so much each and every day,
Just seems like a priceless dream.

You are the reason why we dance the night away
I love your smile more than you know
Your dazzling eyes that make you glow
All I want is for you to know
You make me happy in every way
I don't know what more to say

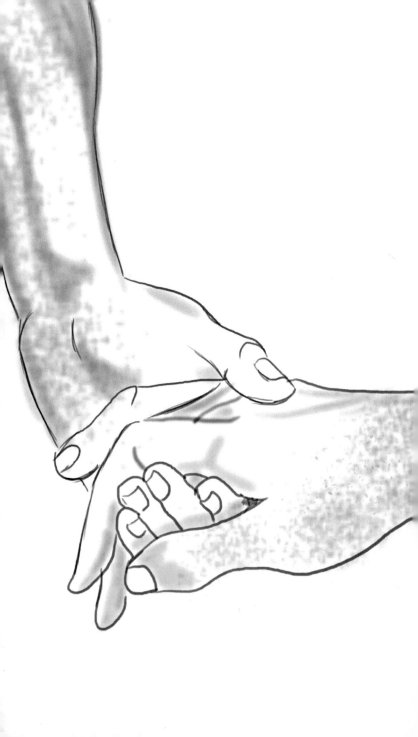

Sweet and simple

Dreams are like angels
They keep the darkness away
The power of love is sweet and simple
This is how they come

The future of love
Is a reckoning force of pleasure?
Across the shadow entwined and divine
This is how you become a luxurious love

Love is a pleasure, love is the light
You hold me close, you keep me at bay
This is how I like you my force of nature,
My wonderful flame

A heart of life, a heart of wonder,
Now you are in the picture
We are young at heart
We both could live a wonderful life
This is how we become an endless romance

Someone I love

I met you in the dark
We danced and drunk all night
At the end, we got stoned
For a minute, I had to pause
To take a deep breath
I could not believe this moment existed
I wished for everyday to be like this one

I thought I'd never find a person like you
Someone that could bring a smile to my face
Someone that I could hold
Someone that made me feel safe

There's not a thing I would change
I would live each day just the way it was
And just so you know
You were that someone
The someone I love

You and me

Open up your mind
I know it is complicated, but we have to try
I know I'm out of my mind
I lay here thinking
Of what we could have been
I drift away to a place where it's just you and me
Where our dreams come true
A place with endless possibilities

All of me belongs to all of you
All I ask is you trust me like I trust you
And let's turn all our endless possibilities into reality

Tell me
Is it just me or have you dreamt this too?

Untitled 3

I'm a random kind of guy
With colours and promises
Somehow all of my doubts suddenly goes away
With you I talk nonsense
You are my kryptonite

Just remember it's just you and me

I'm not sure what life can bring
I'm not sure if dreams can come true
I'm not sure what love is
But I do know that everything is possible
When I'm with you

The war

I left you, was it the pain that drove me to do it
I try to reason with you
At the end I signed up

I traveled with you in my pocket
Like an angel you watched over me
I always made a return

I picked up the phone to call you
You must think I'm a fool
Every time I want to say sorry

The war is coming to an end
The war in my heart
Though my life can still come to an end

I know I shall meet my fate
Somewhere above the clouds
In heaven I will wait until my fate is found

But right now, we have no choice
We have to push on
and ignite the flames of our fate

I know I will be fine with you by my side
So when I'm done I will come back to tell you
I was wrong and I love you

Dearest friend

To my dearest friend you departed this world leaving us all alone
If I could change the world I would
If I could change the harsh times I would
I would travel back to when you left us all and trade my life for yours
Now you're gone, we feel incomplete

My dearest friend
You were my closest of them all
We drunk too much, we partied hard all night long
You treated me like a brother, gave me my first cigar
I wish I could change the past
So you could be here with us, instead of us toasting to your memory

I'm sorry for the arguments
Sorry for the lies
Sorry for the war
Sorry for the loss and most importantly
I'm sorry our friendship was not good enough

I know time has passed and everyone else has forgotten
I know it's too late
There is no way to bring you back
But I will always drink to your memory
My dearest friend

life

I lost something,
something irreplaceable,
a thing of beauty gone forever,
never to see it shine again,
never to make me smile again,
something,
      Truly irreplaceable

Smile

I smile not because I wish to,
Not because I have to,
I don't smile because my heart tells me to,
It is because I want to,
I smile because my heart feels so,
I smile when I see you,
When I'm next to you
And I truly smile because I love you

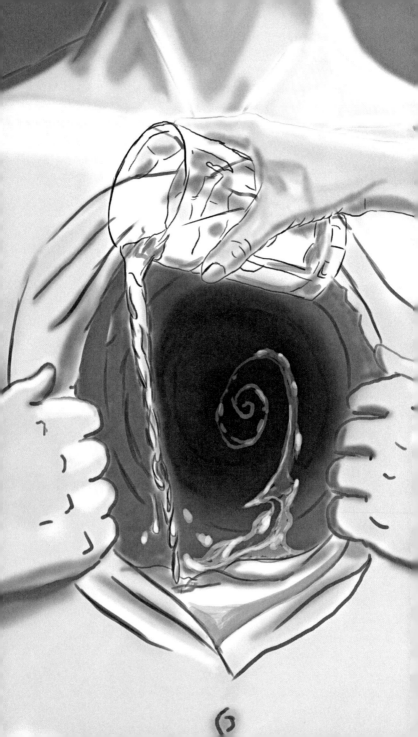

Why

Why is it that when I stand alone
Very alone
My heart feels so empty
Like a vacuum in my chest

But the loneliness floated away
My heart felt life once more
Something I had never felt before
Was it magic or some kind of illusion?
Then I realized it was you

Free to dream

Take my kiss
As your last
I stand no more
Minded I am
Now and forever more

I care not
Years lost
Forever love
Gone and forgotten

To be
Was all I dreamed?
To live
To be seen

Take my hug
As your last
Forever lost
Now and forgotten

A vision you are
To me no more,
I stand and roar
Free I am
No more iron bars

Take these words
As my last
I cared
But no more

This day I'm free
Free to dream
And be me

An old man once said

To be me is not a life you want
I have nothing
All I want is something

I have no family
Maybe this is why, I am here today
No one to love,
No one who cares

I am old and grey
Alone and afraid
There will be no flowers on my grave
To be forever forgotten

Could I have made a better choice?
To give me the life I once dreamed
Was wanting something
Not an authentic dream?

But what now?
What is left?
Just a lonely old man

Don't be like me
Go chase your dreams

I Dream

I dream
A falling dream
A place with hope
A desire to be free
With my last breath
I hope

To be with you is all I dream?
Once again I'm here again
Hope to see and hope to dream
Knowing the pain I will see

Here again I stand
Thinking of when it all began
Remembering you
Remembering me
Knowing where this path will lead

To start again?
Not learning from what was

Is pain worth the distance for love?
Or should I protect my lonely heart?

Wishing on a star

The end comes soon
I'm leaving without you
The stars seem to not shine anymore
She looks at me from afar
But yet she is near
I feel her
I hear her heart
Yet she is far
She looks at me with passion
With each gaze she brings me closer
Yet she is far
I still look to see that one bright star

Fly away and ignite your wings
High above never below
When there is loss there is no replace
Tears of dreams, real tears of sorrow
When you love so hard it remains

When will I tell you?
That I miss you
Hopefully it will be before I meet my end
Could I have locked in your love?
Would you have stayed?

When will I tell you?
That I want to hold you?
Hopefully it will be before time comes to an end
It tears me down to be so far but I know it won't be long
Wait for me I'll be there soon

When will I tell you?
That I love you?
Hopefully before our worlds end
I know your wings are true
I just hope I get mine too

I can't bear to lose you again
I will tell you
...I love you when I see you again

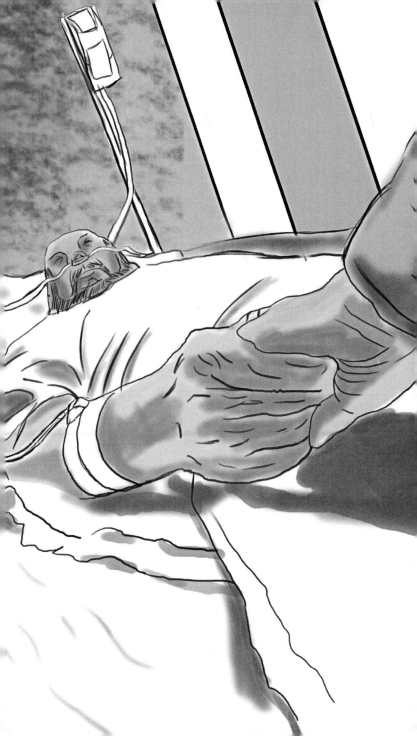

Untitled 4

Whispers of the sea, silent is the key
A moment of truth sealed forever
with every second being timeless
now I feel every heart burning
Hopeful is my spirit, strengthen by my compassion
Because I love you is why I dream

So I can dream of my angel, a miracle you really are
Over the mountains she came where my fate is found
To follow her into the dark and rise into the light
This is our destiny to survive the fight
And to fall deeply and madly in love

The sun has set high above the stars
I now wait
For every moment is treasure I hold
To see the one I love

One hour left and I shall see you soon
Neither of us knew it had been so long
Now everyone knows you'll be coming soon

I wonder how many seconds I have left
so, I can tell you I love you
Over and over again,
I love you very much
Soon I will open my eyes and awaken out of my dreams
To tell you over and over again
            I love you for real not just in my dreams

Not coming home

Do you ever wonder?
Why I have not returned
Why the bed stays cold at night
And why there are no hugs
To keep you warm

I didn't want to leave
But things changed
The dollar bills
The diamond rings
I gave you the extra things

But you changed
From who you were
You weren't the same
You were my childhood sweetheart
now all that is left are the memories

Do you ever wonder?
Where I've gone
And why I haven't returned
But to put it simply
I'm not coming home

I can say
I've seen her

I can say
I've been next to her

I can say
I've touched her

I can truly say
That I have been in love with an Angel.

Do you see?

Do you see the rain of blood fall?
Each tear that falls
Falls for a reason
A teardrop of love
Teardrops of pain
Why do I shed these tears?

Do you see the river of blood flow?
Gushing with great pain
Raging with emotion
Still I continue to hurt myself
Just to make the one I love smile
Why am I doing this?

Do you see
Why I go through this pain?
You are the one I love
Will you ever see?
Or will my tears
Be forever forgotten?

In life

I've loved
I've lost
I've missed
I've been hurt
I've made mistakes
But most of all
        I've lived in life

She fills me with joy

I look into her eyes
Is she real?

She sparkles with light
A presence so bright

Not a day goes by when I don't think of her
An Angel she must be

– Just like that –

Is she really there?
Waiting
Searching
Reaching for the one she loves

Days go by
Chances to show my love
Pass me by
Will this opportunity pass?
Or will I be forgotten

Then one day
I gain the courage
And just like that
I say hello

Friend

I've lost my friend today
But I know he will return,

I'm just glad where he has gone
He will be happy and he is not alone :)

No matter where I go,
Or what I do
You will always be in my heart :)

To all that say

Years have passed
Nothing has changed
I have little or no money
Nothing but pain

To watch and listen
To all those who judge and compare
My heart feels heavy
A burden I bare

This is the life I lead
Do you feel my pain?
I hear it calling
It whispers to me

Failure I am to those around me
No one is proud of me
I failed to see my dreams
Should I just now lay down this pen?

Follow your heart (but count on me)

You are always on my mind and thoughts
Your smile, your dazzling eyes
My gaze is always on you

You make me happy
When you're here
Follow your heart and be here

If you don't yet know?
Trust your heart and ask me
You can never go wrong with me

Left and forgotten

I wait for her,
To give me a sign
Maybe a smile
But I receive nothing

Every time I see her,
My heart skips a beat
I'm filled with joy
Happiness and care

I gaze at the stars,
Like we did
Hand in hand
Making our wish

Now I look alone
Why do you hate me so much?
We shared those words
Only to take it all away

There was no love in your heart
That's the only truth that shows
And if I'm lucky I'll die with a broken heart
                    Left alone and forgotten

Days

Days go by slowly
My heart feels so empty,
It beats ever so slowly

I count the days of your return,
All I have left is the memory of that perfect moment that left
me mesmerized

But wherever I may be and wherever you may be, I hope you are
happy
Your happiness is my smile, your smile is my happiness and you
bring the light out of me, to help me shine and give me that one
feel that is untamable.

Meaning of love

I finally understood what true love meant...
love meant that you care for another person's happiness
more than your own,
no matter how painful the choices will be.

Drunk I

Why do you drink?
You have no reason
Yet you drink
A fool you've become
A pain to others

Why is it a need?
The addiction
The hope for more

Do you really need
Hopeless dreams
A bottle gives?

Do you find solitude?
At the end of a bottle
Does the last drop suffice?

I think you choose
To give pain to others
To leave your life at the end of a bottle

Drunk II

Fallen to the ground
To lift you I could not
Can you see
People are watching
Why do you embarrass me?

Look at me
You're such a case
While you fall apart
I hide the bottles
That causes the pain

Can't you see
I'm wrapped in a blanket of pain
This hurts me more than you think
To break free
Is an impossible pain

To let you drown your sorrows
Is where I may be free
I can't hide
All the bottles

Can't you see
I'm wrapped in a blanket of pain too
But I do not drown my sorrows
Embrace life
Fight what you can't see
Together we can be free

Drunk III

You say you're upset
You're fed up of life
Yet I stand here to help

You push me away
Call me names
Don't talk

The only thing that helps is a bottle
To destroy your empire is what you only wish
Advance from your own blood you do not seek

What more can I say?
What more can I do?
I try and try

All we have is what's left
Don't destroy your legacy
Over a bottle

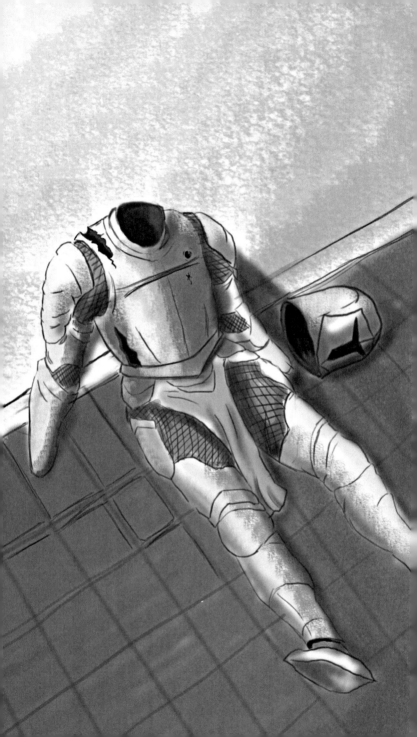

Wondering man

What they did to me
Killing me slowly inside
They took it from me
My passion
My soul
My heart
All that is left is this empty shell
Of a wondering man

Every day I look
Every day I wonder
How did I get here?
I did so much for everyone
I protected everyone
But no one protected me

There were things in place
To help someone like me
But the rules were broken
Because the colour of my skin
Is this the world we live in now?
A world of pain

To lick some ass to be favored
As King
All I am is human
I will do no such thing
Because I am the wondering man

Sometimes I feel like just ending it
I feel like just letting go
Sometimes I feel like just dying

Maybe I should
Life is not the same
She is not the same
Nothing is the same

It's time to say goodbye

Safe

You think you are all safe
You dream of hope
Hope is just a lie,
A figment of your imagination
But the truth will set you free.

You are truly

Unimaginable
Priceless
Miraculous
Angelic
Unspeakable
Adorable
Lovely
Sexy
Sweet
Nice
Beautiful
Honest
Romantic
Interesting
Attractive
Precious
TO me

For the rest of our lives
I believed my dreams could make me fly
I hoped
I lived
Only to be torn apart

I pushed the boundaries
I heard all the no's
The rejection
The lies
But I carried on
With each breath I took
I moved forward
To better myself
To show you I could

Throughout the years
I felt the pain
That you all gave me
Not once did you help me

I want you to know
That with each laugh
With each joke
With all the discrimination
It made me feel low
It made me feel sad
I felt hopeless
I felt all I had achieved
Was for nothing

To all those who laughed at me
To all those who never supported me
My teachers, My friends

Remember now I am better
Better off now without you
Because I am proud to be me

The sun has finally set,
Darkness had finally crept in
All that is left are the whispers from my dying breath

All I am is me
Soon to be free
All that is left are the last whispers of my dying breath

For reasons to be, life is not to be
For you to see, for you to be
Is the reason for me to leave

Love to be was the reason to be
With you I would be a reason to see
Smile to be was the reason to breathe
To know what will be is to cheat destiny

To know what we can achieve was good enough for me
For you to see is for me to believe
The life I lead was not a dream
You are for me, an angel you may be
My whispers are free, for you to see

Be Free

Only in dark there is light,
Only in dying life
Brightness takes flight
Through the empty sky.

Only in death there is life
Only in light there is dark
Only in living life
Darkness takes flight
Through the unemptied sky

Both are so
Both are now
We are what we are
Life and darkness
Joint at the bone

In death you are free
May we live?
Only to be chained
To fight
To be free

Sisters

My sisters are the best,
I've never appreciated everything they have done for me
Since I was little
Helping me with my homework
Taking me shopping,
Making sure I had what they never had
And even until now
Giving me advice
Making sure I'm ok
I am so grateful to have them.
I just want them to know
I'm thankful for everything they do and I love them both
so much,
even though I don't say it enough

Mother

I wake the same, cold is my bed, and silence is in the air,
Roughness lingers in the back, as dry as it can be. I get
pushed out of my bed to get dressed,

Every day I wake up, it is the same. I get up out of my
cold bed feeling the roughness in the back of my dry
throat and get dressed. Like always, my mother was
gone leaving every day at 4 am, 12 hours a day to support
me and make the house run on her one pay cheque. I
hope to change this, I hope that she would never have to
work again, that she could stand tall and be proud of me
some day.

A star once said, I wonder what it would feel like to be human, to be free, to wonder and live your dreams. I wish I could fly among the stars towards my destiny. To be free and see the great wonders through space and time, to hope is just a dream; I am what I am, a simple lonely star stuck in my dreams.

My life is in transit
It is lost
I look for my shadow
My soul
The one in clink of the missing piece

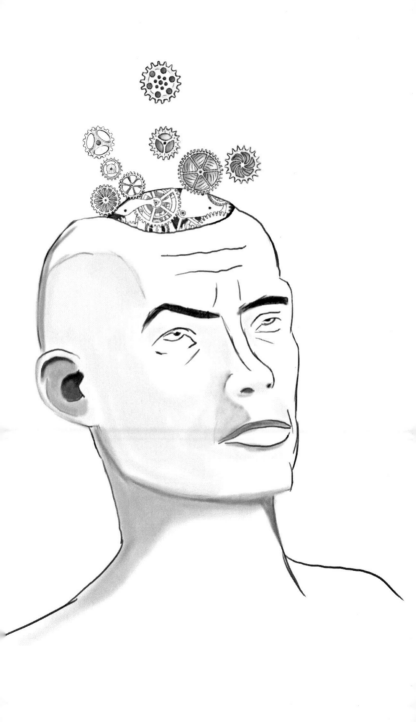

Superior Trust

Kochanie

All this time, I still wonder why I cannot move on
    We don't talk any more; I sit in our spot looking across the
    sea, hoping you will appear to tell me, you love me,
    I feel so empty
    To not be able to feel your heart intertwine with mine
It leaves me broken,
    You could have tried,
You could have spoken to my heart Kochanie,
    to throw it all away over the phone
Was your mistake?

Tell your mom it was nice to meet her,
    I would have been proud to be a part of her family
    And tell her we would have rocked the New Year with a
    diamond ring.
        I tried to justify the situation
                Every time I tried to make you happy
                        You went south
                    It was never enough
        Yet I still sit and hope
                Only to suffer alone

I loved you dangerously more than your enemies
I kissed you passionately more than you needed
　　　To inspire your dreams was my destiny
I'm just a sucker for your blue eyes
　　　We lived on the edge, with honesty

I did not realize
I wasted my time
You fell for all the lies
　　　　He told you he could treat you better than I could
You accepted openly
　　　　Left me to suffer
To feel the pain, was my endless desire
A pain I never expected to experience
　　　　　　You just made me suffer
You're just cold hearted

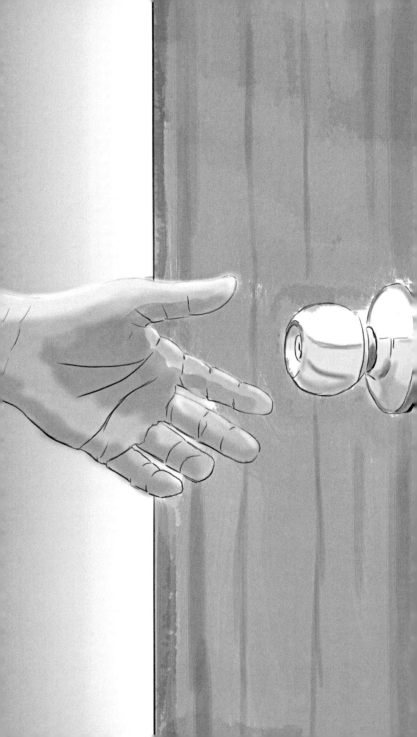

So much to lose
I don't want to be here no more
I can't stand this pain
I wished to see it go
To take the easy way out
Is the best way?

I'm losing my mind because of you
I had so much planned
So much to do
Was so proud
We were almost there
Just a few more steps

I said, I love you
I knew it was going to hurt
I ignored the signs
Did not seek the truth
As you kept me waiting

I loved you crazily
Yet I held in the pain
I felt you were choking me
I guess, I was a sucker for pain

I loved you imaginably
You kept me waiting
I did not realize
How you made me suffer

I loved you dangerously
I did not see the other guy
A pain I feel until this day
You kept me waiting
While you were with him

I sold everything you gave
I'm not afraid to look and say
I'm moving on

I won't do anything to make you love me
All I will do is live my life and watch until you see
The mistake you made

Everyone knows I was not the fool
I know I can treat you better than anyone
There is nothing I will do, you will see your mistake

When you look back you will realize, what we had was better
than anything you had, by then it will be too late.

When you walked into the room
Everything changed
I remember the light bouncing of your blonde hair
I watched to see if you looked at me
Would you brave the unknown to say hello?

I saw you still wear the chain I gave you
Maybe some love remains
Or do you wear it because it's a Tiffani
Misled I am
Not knowing if there is a
What if?

Wake up
See the reality
You've seen him beat his wife
But we say nothing
That's life

No one reports the abuse
We are all afraid
There are more of us
Together we are stronger
To fight our pain

To show them we are not afraid

If you like the way you look
Then maybe you should go and love yourself
He doesn't love you
Like Batman vs. Superman
Martha was the key

He does not like you nor do you
Because if you like the way
how Martha plays with your mind
Then you should go and love yourself

I need you
I need you right now
Why do you not listen to my cries?

The life I lead is a life of misery
Why do you not grant my wishes?
They say you are everywhere
Then you see my pain

Help me to believe in you
I need you now
Don't let me down
Save me from my misery

I thought I had been hurt before
But no one had hurt me more than you did
Now I need someone to save my life
To bring me back

I thought I could not feel pain when I was with you
I was wrong to have believed in you.
I have to pick up the pieces
With no one to comfort me

I need to get you out of my head
I need to pick up these pieces
Show the world I'm back

I must be better
Stronger
Braver

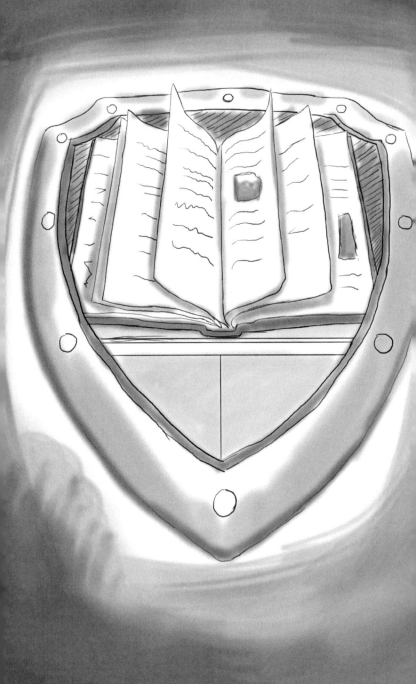

Knowledge is power, to defeat your enemies
Love is the power, to defeat your heart
I was not your enemy
I was your lover and you betrayed me
Used and abused for your games
There was no love in your heart for me
Your cold heart of stone
Could never experience love

The world can be a hard place
Don't let it defeat you
Don't let it bring you down
Don't carry the world on your shoulders

Go ahead
Go beyond
Show the world you are more
Fight it with kindness
Prove him wrong and become what you were born to be

I'm afraid to see you
I want you closer
To hold and tell you what I want

I steer in a bottle,
Looking not knowing if it was enough,
To conceal my pain

It will never be enough
No bottle can cure me from you
You are a pledge to stay

Come on

Can't you see?
He is playing you

Can't you see?
He is using you

When will you learn?
That he does not love you

You do not listen
Even when you can see the truth

When will it be too late in the name of love,
To see the truth behind his brown eyes?

I got this electric
Flowing through my body
It's placed by a unique thing called Love

Do you feel it too?
I can't seem to shake this feeling

You have the right to remain silent
Would you stay by my side?
If I took a step back
To support you
Would you judge me because you have a better job?

If I lost it all today
Would you judge me or stay by my side?
Even though I supported you
And gave you the time you needed
Would you still stay?

All I want is you, as you are
I need a girl who would always be by my side
If you took this job
You have the right to remain silent
Does this mean you will run
And leave me behind?

Would you still love me the same
Or would you turn your back?
If you earn more than me
Would you truly stay?

The truth is I supported you through your job, waited ......
Just because you earned more than me,
You ran away because someone else told you to

I always wonder after all these years
Would you like to meet?
To feel young and be free
Like we once use to be
Would you like to meet?
And talk about the old times
To smile like we once did
To feel good as we did,
To tell you what I've been up to
Take my hand and see where it goes
So what do you say?

I was blinded by love
To drink from the fountain of youth
Was my curse?

To feel this everlasting love
Was buried deep into my destiny
Time could not heal this pain

All I could do was never give up
I climb so high
To see if I can find another

No one was like her
She could never be replaced
My angel, my love

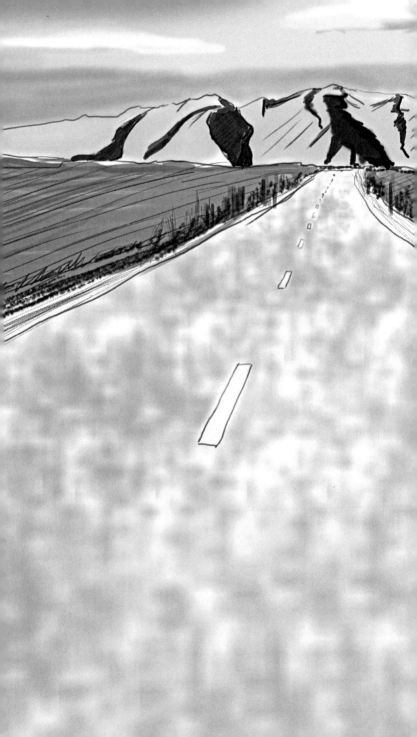

So it begins
Life on the road
All alone

What wonder may I see?
On my great journey to inner peace

What would I do without your smile?
What would I do without your touch?
How many times do I have tell you
A vision you are?

I love all your imperfections
Because I love all of you
I am nothing without you
Because you complete me

My mystical journey
Always leads me to you
Even now when I should stay away

Don't give up

I think it is so cute
How you listen to your fake friends
They don't want the best for you

Oh my god
Look at that face
So surprised,
Did you think this would never come out?
That people wouldn't find out about my pain

Today I start my life with a blank canvas
I could scream, shout, and cry
That won't bring you back or ease my pain
I am a gentleman

My mate Carla told me to grow up
Be better
And guess what
I did

I never forgave you
You were a party girl
You told me you were going to a party
With another man

I did not know
You were with this man
While you were with me
I did not know you were capable of these things

You were meant to be the one

New chapter Bella

Days became months
Months became years
The pain seems to stay
It does not fade
nor does it heal
It lingers and waits

She gave me this pain
This everlasting pain
In my heart
Forever more to stay
Waiting to strike

I feel so broken
Unable to be fixed

I seem to look
But I do not find

Shattered I am
Searching for all the pieces
Where to look
When will I find it?

Incomplete I feel
Lost with no words
Hoping someone will find
my missing pieces

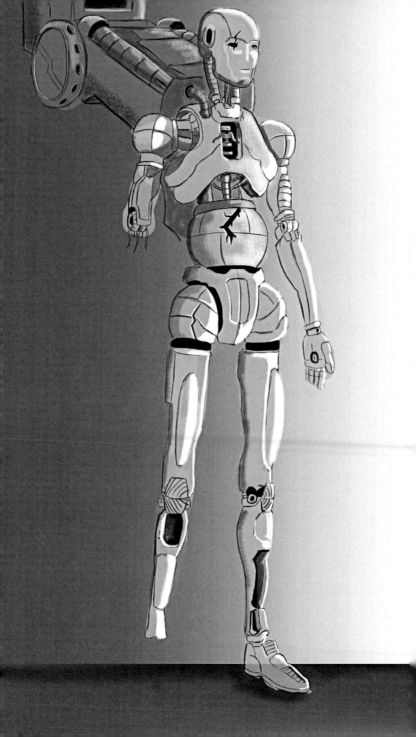

I'm broken
I suffered the most
The endless pain
People told me
But I did not listen
Clouded I was by my own judgment

Never thought it could happen to me,
Advice I gave people
Thinking I knew it all
The truth behind it all
I knew nothing at all

Suffer I will
Until my dying days
The pain I feel will stay
Buried deep within my soul

It hurts me to think
She is with him

It hurts me to talk
When she is with him

When I think of her smile it makes me happy
Followed I am by the pain, that I will never see that smile again

When I think about all the things we did, it makes me happy,
Followed I am by the pain that I will never do those things again.

When I think about the special days and events we planned, it
makes me happy.
Followed I am by the pain that I will never do those things again.

When I see her pictures it makes me happy, followed I am by the
pain that I did not take them or like those things again.

It all belongs to him now

All I'm left with is this pain

When I see a blonde
I feel this pain
When I see a baby
I feel this pain
When I think of her with him
I feel this pain
When I think about her
I feel this pain
When I see a girl with blue eyes
I feel this pain
When I talk about her
I feel this pain

If I feel all this pain, why does she not feel anything?

Why could you not tell me?

You must have known you didn't love me
Seemed like you used me for five years

You must have known you didn't see a future with me
To tell me after five years

All I did was love you
To tell me you didn't feel the same way like how I felt for you
What went wrong in the five years?

To leave me on the sidewalk
With no answer to my questions
To leave me waiting to know if we are still to be

Three months passed
No text
No call
What did I do?
To be treated like this

The love we once shared
Meant nothing to you
Even though I stood by you
Supported you
I gave you space to complete your dreams

But it was not enough
I was never enough
To complete you

However, I want you to know
Even though I waited
Trusted you
Gave you the space you needed,
And hope we would once be

You completed me in everyway
because you were enough for me

She

She isn't coming back
Whispered my heart

She controls my faith
Said my brain

She cheated and used you
Said my friends

Give her space
Said my family

Alone I will be
Forever she was my destiny

My tears leave a burning trail
The pain caused
The pain gained
What was, was not meant to be
To see the light sooner was just a hopeless dream

Darkness is coming
In the form of love
Light is no longer the key to sanctuary

People say she will break you
Consume you and take your soul
You will fall ever so deep into her blue eyes

Giving her everything
Only for her to leave you with nothing

A hollow heart
Sealed and locked away

Never to dream
Never to hope
Or smile again

                    Which took years to fill

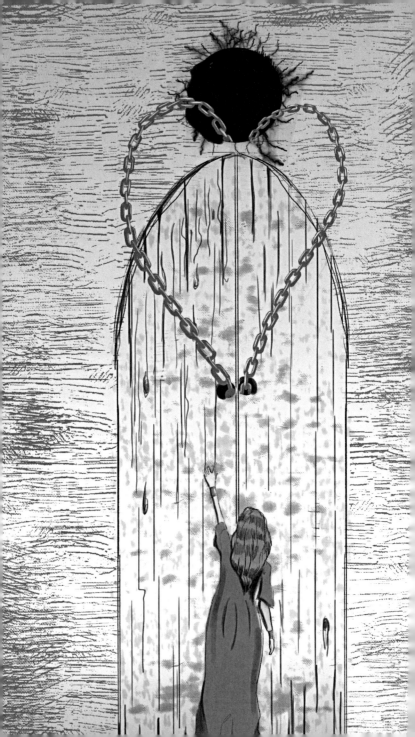

I feel sad
Broken I was before
I shared the pain of my past
How hard it was for me to trust

You knew my all
How afraid I was
To be in love once again
To be hurt
Would lead me to my death

Is this what you seek?
To give me hope
Only to take it
To make promises
Only to break them

Was it your plan?
To lead me for years
Only to leave me
By cheating

How dare you lie
You asked for space
Only to cheat

How did I not know?
The signs were so clear
You changed the way you kissed me

I hoped you would see
That I was worth every penny
But your heart desired something else

Your heart desired
The darkness

You chose to break me
Hurt me

To lie was your goal
To cheat was your destiny

I just did not know
I could not foresee
What was awaiting me

People said you were no good
But I stood my ground
Defended you with my all

I broke the rules
Defined the odds
To prove to them all they were wrong

But they were right
Once a cheat
Always a cheat

So maybe this time your new man should put a ring on
your finger

I protected you
Defended you
Loved you

In return

You hurt me
Lied to me
Broke me

To me you are dead

To hurt me was your wrong
To love me was your right
To lie to me was your decision

So when people ask me about you
I will say wherever she is
I hope she finds peace

Because I never hurt her
I always loved her
I never lied

And my Bella died the day she broke my heart

16/03/1990
28/08/2016

I control my emotions
I try to stay brave
It is hard
Yet I still remain

Family and friends
Feel my pain
Time will heal
My everlasting broken heart

All I have to do is remain
Why did God make this pain?

Situations come and go
This one stays until the end
It seems to not leave me
I've never felt a pain like this before

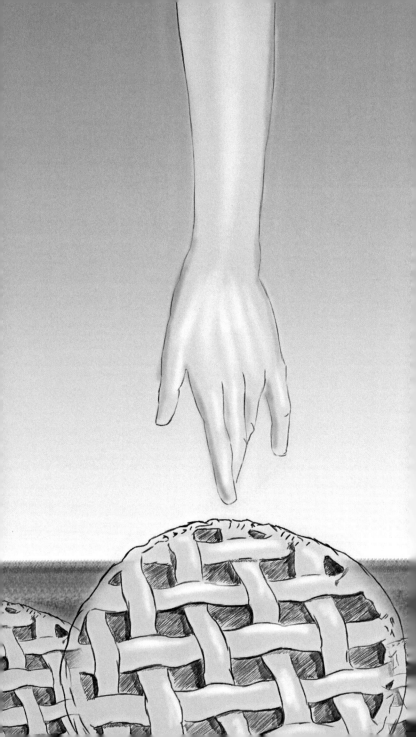

How easy it was for you to move on
You do not look back
At the love we once shared

I hope you would see the new light in me
You did not
Nor want to
Because you had your finger in another pie

Dad was right

He always told me
I did not listen
I hoped to prove him wrong
As love was present

You use to say
I would be the one to go
What went wrong?
I stayed
Yet you left within the time frame

Guess Dad was right
Six years he gave
Until you'll leave he said
Guess he did not trust the blonde hair

You felt no pain
In the decision you made
I guess it shows that you have no soul
And a heart of stone

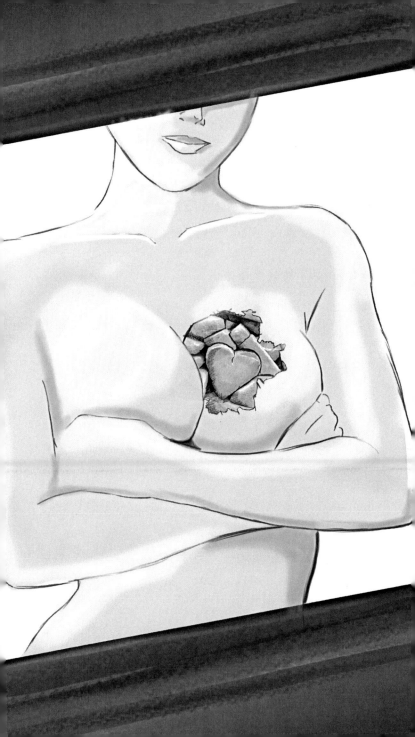

My Bella was a treat
She had to join the pxxxxx
To become a cheat

How I wonder
Will the law protect us?
If full of cheats

How they get manipulated
To live a life of lies
It will be their demise

The words that stay in my mind
I'm dating someone
I waited two weeks
I told you I did not feel the same
I told you we would talk later
I don't see a future with you

Only if she knew what Martha did

Martha

Martha your friend
Lied till the end
Created a world without me

Only if you knew the truth
That lay beyond your blonde hair
On how fake your friends are

He and Martha
Planned it all
Until the end

Blinded you are by the fake relationships
You hold
Created by Martha and her friend

The only truth
That remains until the end
Is my love was real until the end

If you're wondering what I'm talking about ask Martha

It was like the light went off, I stood in darkness and waited
It changed everything
She was no more
My Bella had gone

All that was left was an empty shell